Sir Malcolm Arn
a life in pictures

With a foreword by

Anthony Meredith

Compiled by Paul Harris and Rupert Burchett

We are most grateful to the following for the use of their photographs:

Katherine Arnold, Robert Arnold, Sheila Arnold, John Carewe, Tony Cooper, Brian and Mary Charlton, Anthony Day, Mavis Emery, Jenny Gregory, Annetta Hoffnung, Alan Poulton, Penny Pullen, Mike Purton, Jill Smallshaw and Basil Tschaikov.

We should be grateful to be told of any omissions to the above list. Any such oversights will be rectified in subsequent editions.

A percentage of royalties from this book will be donated to The Musicians Benevolent Fund.

ISBN 978-0-9552473-3-0

QT 101   Malcolm Arnold: a life in pictures

© 2008 by Queen's Temple Publications, 15 Mallard Drive, Buckingham, MK18 1GJ
www.qtpublications.co.uk

First published in 2008 by Queen's Temple Publications.
Printed in Scotland by Spartan Press

FOREWORD

The single-minded devotion which Paul Harris gives to the Arnold cause could not be better exemplified than in his determination to publish this small book of photographs, celebrating the Arnold Festival of 2008, the third annual event held under the auspices of the Royal & Derngate, Northampton.

During the past year or so Paul and I have been working on a biography of Sir Richard Rodney Bennett, just fifteen years Sir Malcolm's junior. Bennett spent two formative years in Paris as Pierre Boulez's pupil before developing his own very personal serial style of composition, so, to put it all into its proper context, Paul and I have been listening to much post-war avant-garde music. It has reminded us most forcefully just what an iconoclast Sir Malcolm was in pursuing Mahlerian and Sibelian tonality at that time; and what huge audacity and remarkable strength of character he showed in going his own way and saying 'bugger-the-lot-of-them'. Something of the sheer pugnacity of the man surely comes out in several of the photographs in this book? Here are the Seven Ages not just of a great composer but of *a singular personality*. That last photograph of all, for example, speaks volumes.

Of course Sir Malcolm paid heavily for the sin of cocking many a roguish snook at the establishment, and, although he's long since come in from the cold, he still struggles for fitting recognition in the professional concert repertoire. In just thirteen years comes the centenary of his birth. Will the Arnold Festival by then have become a major landmark in the British musical calendar? Will the 7th Symphony have been acknowledged as one of the great jewels in the European symphonic crown? Will the 5th and the 4th and the 3rd and the 2nd have been heard again in the Royal Albert Hall? And what about the enigmatic 1st and 8th, and the even more enigmatic 9th? Meanwhile, how many of those brilliant concertos will have been embraced by the country's major soloists? Will, in short, some of the greatest and most life-enhancing British music of the twentieth century have finally prevailed?

In the meantime, as we ponder the imponderable, we can but rejoice in the Third Arnold Festival, held in the town of his birth. Thank you, the Royal & Derngate! And thank you, Paul!

Anthony Meredith

For the full story of Sir Malcolm's life, read *Malcolm Arnold: Rogue Genius*, published by Omnibus Press and written by Anthony Meredith & Paul Harris.

Aged 6 months

With brother Philip and father,
William Arnold (Pappy)

Below: Family c.1923.
Aubrey and Pappy
(top row); Philip, Ruth,
Malcolm, Annie (Nan)
and Clifford (seated)

Above: at the beach in
Bournemouth with Philip, 1922

Above: with Ruth
at the Broads

Above, right and
below: with Philip
at Fairview

Right: with Philip and Clifford

Left: with Philip at Eaglehurst Sports Day, County Ground, 1926

Above and left: on holiday with the family, c.1927

Above and below:
with the family

Right: with
Philip on
holiday in
Belgium

Below: with Aubrey, Ruth, Clifford (who appears to be holding a
hammer!) and Philip in the garden at Fairview

Student Days
1938 - 41

Below: with Pappy
and Philip at
Craigmore

Above: with Pappy

Left: with Pappy, Ruth and Nan on the promenade at Llandudno

Left: with Aubrey, Ruth, Clifford and Philip

Left: with Philip and Ruth

9

Above and below: with family

Above and below: the young trumpeter with the LPO at the Proms, 1942

Aabove: with Nan and Sheila on Northampton racecourse

Orpheum

GOLDERS GREEN

MUSICAL CULTURE LIMITED present

NEW LONDON ORCHESTRA

BACH: Brandenburg Concerto No. 3 in G

BRITTEN: Four Folk Songs

SHOSTAKOVITCH: Concerto for Piano, Trumpet and Strings

BEETHOVEN: Symphony No. 3 in E flat (Eroica)

Conductor - **ALEC SHERMAN**

Solo Pianoforte **MEWTON-WOOD**

Solo Trumpet - **MALCOLM ARNOLD**

Solo Tenor - **PETER PEARS**

SUNDAY FEBRUARY 14 at 7

PROGRAMME AND NOTES - SIXPENCE

The trumpet virtuoso, 1944

14876218 Private Arnold, M
2 Platoon, B Company
Royal East Kent Regiment,
1944

Left: with
Denis Egan
in 1946

Right: with fellow
Northampton composers
Edmund Rubbra and
William Alwyn

Left and below: on
holiday in Soay

Above: a portrait
taken in 1948

Above: with some friends during
the Mendelssohn Scholarship
period, Rome, 1948

Right: with
Jack Thurston
(wearing hat) and
other National Youth
Orchestra staff, 1948

Below: rehearsing the
National Youth Orchestra
brass section, 1948

Below: rehearsing his
first symphony, 1949

Above: with baby Robert,
Sheila and Katherine

Above and below:
with Katherine

Above: with Ruth, baby
Jenny and Charles
Dickens

Below: with musical friends,
clockwise: Judy Hill,
Richard Adeney, William
Waterhouse and Livia Gollancz

With Katherine, Robert and Sheila

The composer in
the early 1950s

Right: with
the score of
Beckus, 1953

The young conductor

Above left: with Katherine in Southbourne, 1951. Above right: the family in 1953.

Right: Family Portrait, 1959
Clockwise: Pappy, Katherine, MA, Lizzie Witts, Sheila, Robert, Sally Anne and Doll

Below: with Bridge on the River Kwai Oscar, 1958

Below: Denbigh Gardens

Left: coaching a
brass ensemble,
1952

Right: working with the
girls of St. Trinian's
on the film set, 1954

Left and below:
working with young
musicians, 1958

Composer at
work, late 1950s

Below: Dorothy Payne, MA's
secretary, 1957-1965

Left: preparing for the Hoffnung Festival with Sheila and Pauline del Mar on vacuum cleaner and floor polisher, 1956

Above and below: with Gerard Hoffnung in 1959

PROGRAMME NOTE

Grand Overture . . . . Malcolm Arnold

Mr. Arnold is widely known as perhaps the most melodious of our distinguished younger composers. It is not surprising, therefore, that in this new work he has called freely on the familiar yet unique lyrical gifts of Hoover Cleaners and Floor Polishers. Their accompaniment to the second subject of the overture is, indeed, a sublime moment of functional art. With a series of brilliant *glissandi*, this Hoover quartet makes a remarkable contribution to orchestral texture. And their farewell, as each of these ingenious instruments in turn becomes silent, is one of the most moving experiences in modern music.

This is a great occasion. For the song of the Hoover, so dear to women all over the world, has at last been given a worthy place in musical history.

HOOVER LIMITED

By Appointment
Suppliers of Musical Instruments to The Hoffnung
Musical Festival

Left: with Larry Adler at the first performance of the Concerto for Harmonica and Orchestra, Royal Albert Hall, 1954

Above: with Harold Parfitt, John Kuchmy and Anatole Fistoulari at Chatham Town Hall, 1956

Below: broadcasting in 1959

Below: writing the Guitar Concerto with Julian Bream, 1959

Left: with Carol Reed (right), 1956

With Katherine and Robert
on their family holiday to
Saas Fee, near Zermatt,
1959

Left: taking the applause after the first performance of the 5th Symphony, Cheltenham Town Hall, 1961

Right: on a visit to Prague, 1961

Right: with Menuhin, 1962

Left: on his trip to the USSR, meeting the Union of Soviet Composers in Moscow, 1963

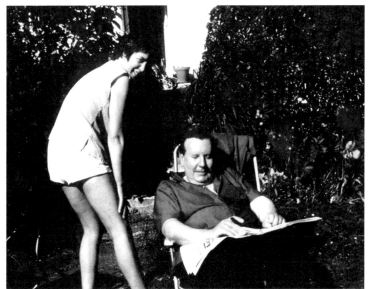

Above and left: with
Isobel at Padstow in
the early 1960s

Left: in the
Farmer's Arms,
St. Merryn,
1966

Below: walking
on the cliff at
St Agnes, 1966

Left: May Day
in Padstow,
1967

Above: at Trevelyan College, Durham University for
the first performance of the Trevelyan Suite, 1967

Left: with the Duke
of Kent and Isobel
at the launch of the
Padstow Lifeboat
(boat and music),
1967

Right: with Sir Arthur Bliss
1967

Left: conducting the
orchestra of the
European Summer
School for Young
Musicians (dir.
John Davies) in the
2nd Symphony,
Vienna 1967

Below: conducting the Cornish Youth Band in the Little Suite No.2 for
Brass Band, 1967

Left and right: with John Amis, 1968

Left: conducting the Cornish Dances, 1968

Right: conducting the recording of the score of William Walton's Battle of Britain, 1969

Below: the Bard of the Gorsedd, 1969

Above: on
Padstow Quay,
1968

Left: 1969

Above: with Cyril Smith and Phyllis Sellick, rehearsing the Concerto for Two Pianos, Sir Arthur Bliss looking on, 1969

Below: publicity photograph for the record sleeve of the Concerto

With
Deep Purple,
conducting
Jon Lord's
Concerto for
Rock Band and
Orchestra,
1969

1970

Left: with Mr and
Mrs Humphrey
Searle, 1971

Right: in
pensive mood,
early 1970s

Above: with
Edward, 1970

Right: with
Edward and
Isobel

Below: with Katherine,
Edward and Isobel, 1972

Below: with Edward
in Cornwall, 1970

William Walton's 70ᵗʰ birthday
celebrations, 1972

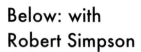

Below: with
Nicholas Maw

Below: with
Robert Simpson

Conducting in 1973

Left: in the garden at Meadowcroft, Dublin, 1974

Right: with Isabel

Above and below: with Terence Emery and David Drew discussing Three Musketeers, 1975

Above and above right:
in the early 80s

Right: with
Mary Charlton and
Alan Poulton, touring

Left: with grandson
Sebastian, 1981

Left: receiving an Honorary Doctorate from the University of Durham, 1982, with Chancellor Margot Fonteyn

Below: receiving a Fellowship of the Royal College of Music from HM Queen Elizabeth the Queen Mother, 1983

Left: with Brian Charlton, outside Elgar's house, May 1983

Below: with Sir David Willcocks and Sir Michael Tippett at the 100th anniversary of the Royal College of Music, 1983

Left: with Gordon
Hunt (oboe) and
Norman del Mar

The recording of
four of the
concertos in
Bournemouth,
September 1984

Left: with Norman del Mar
and John Wallace (trumpet)

Below: with
Janet Hilton

Left: with
Alan Civil

Left: being interviewed by Sheridan Morley for BBC2 at Bunwell Manor Hotel, 1984

Right: with HRH The Princess Royal receiving the Wavendon Award (John Dankworth and Ned Sherrin in attendance), 1985

Left: with Michala Petri 1986

With Julian Lloyd Webber

Left: with Sir Edward Downes at his 65th birthday recording, 1986

Left: as composer in residence at the Perth Festival, 1987

Right: towards the end of the 80s

46

Left and below left: with Charles Groves at the first play through of his 9th Symphony, 1988

Right: with Charles Groves and Dennis Simons at the BBC Philharmonic performance of the 9th Symphony in Manchester, BBC Studio 7, 1992

Left: with the Fine Arts Brass Quintet, on the way to rehearse the 2nd Brass Quintet, 1989

Above and left: Malcolm
at 70.

Left: with Ross Pople at
his 70th birthday party

Above and Left: Conducting the LPO performing the 4th Symphony, 1990

Below: conducting Julian Bream and the English Chamber Orchestra

Left: conducting the Padstow Lifeboat

Norfolk in
the '90s

Left: having just
received his
knighthood at
Buckingham Palace,
1993

Below: with conductor
Andrew Penny and Alan Smale,
leader of the National Orchestra
of Ireland, recording the Nine
Symphonies

Below: with Vernon Handley, 1994

Right: interviewed for Radio Oxford University by Sam Edenborough celebrating his 75th birthday in 1996

Left: holiday caricature, 1996

Below: receiving his Fellowship of the Royal Northern College of Music with HRH The Duchess of Kent, 1997

Above and left: with Simon Rattle at a performance of Little Suite No. 2 by 4000 children in the Birmingham National Indoor Arena, with Anthony Day, 1998

Below: with John Wallace

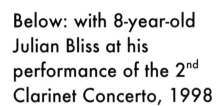

Below: with 8-year-old Julian Bliss at his performance of the 2nd Clarinet Concerto, 1998

Above: at his 80th birthday concert in Norwich
with Anthony Day, Claire Watters (soprano),
Jonathan Howse (clarinet) and Benjamin Davey
(piano) 2001

Below: at the Royal Academy of Arts as
part of The Queen's Golden Jubilee
celebrations, with Malcolm Williamson,
2003

Right: being greeted by
HM The Queen and
HRH The Duke of Edinburgh
with Anthony Day at the
Prom at the Palace in 2003

Left: receiving the ISM award
for services to music in 2005.
Above with Anthony Day and
Paul Harris. Below with
Ken Hÿtch and Robert Lloyd.

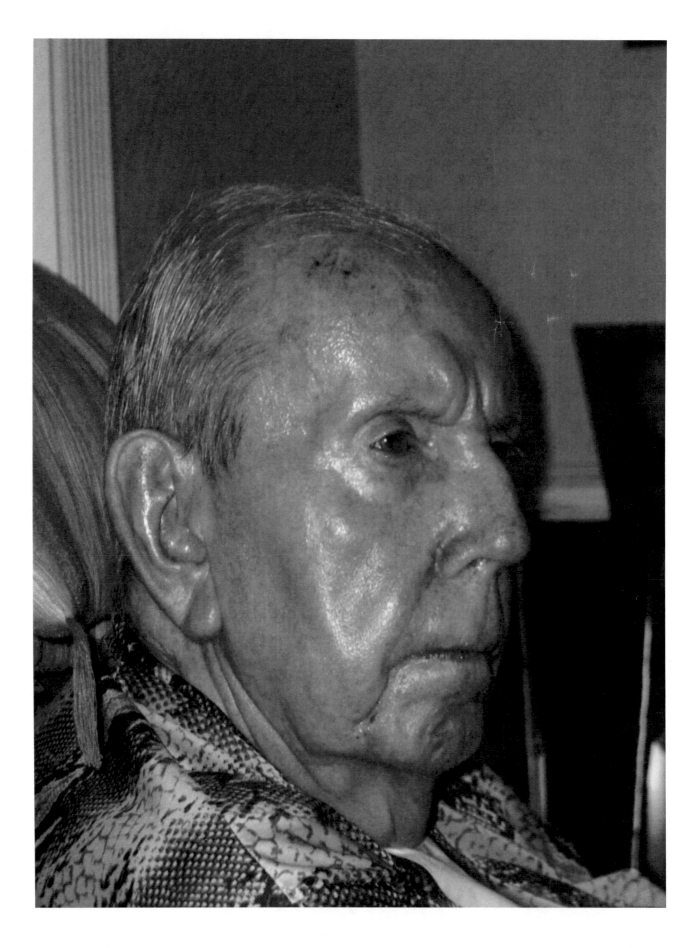

Sir Malcolm Arnold in 2006